ROCK & ROLL
HALL OF FAMERS

Elton John

KATHERINE WHITE

the rosen publishing group's
rosen
central

Published in 2003 by The Rosen Publishing Group, Inc.
29 East 21st Street, New York, NY 10010

Copyright © 2003 by The Rosen Publishing Group, Inc.

First Edition

Library of Congress Cataloging-in-Publication Data

White, Katherine, 1975–
Elton John / by Katherine White.– 1st ed.
p. cm. — (Rock & roll hall of famers)
Includes discography (p.   ), bibliographical references
(p.   ), and index.
ISBN 0-8239-3641-4 (lib. bdg.)
1. John, Elton—Juvenile literature. 2. Rock musicians—
England—Biography—Juvenile literature. [1. John,
Elton. 2. Musicians. 3. Rock music.] I. Title. II. Series.
ML3930.J58 W47 2002
782.42166c'092—dc21
                                        2001008219

Manufactured in the United States of America

CONTENTS

Elton John has been writing hit songs and electrifying audiences for the past three decades.

Introduction

The life of rock and roll began many years ago. It came forth because of a melting pot—a blend of different types of music—and has changed as each new musician played it his or her own way.

Just like in all forms of art, there are those musicians who are considered to be the best. They excel because their talent and expertise extends beyond that of their peers. Their music becomes the sound track to the moments in your life that you remember. Their albums are the ones you buy and listen to repeatedly. You look to their music for inspiration, understanding, and good times. Their performances are the ones you not only stand in line for but also the ones you count down the days until you attend. You love their music as much as they love making it.

Few musicians actually reach this kind of fame, as only a select few remain in the forefront of the public eye, producing music that not only they love but that you love, too. These are the musicians that become legends.

Elton John is one of those musicians. Since the beginning of his musical career in 1970, he has remained an innovative force in music. For thirty years, at least one of his songs has been on the *Billboard* Hot 100 at any given time. At times, he has had two or three songs on the chart at once. His life is an interesting one, and not only because of his music, though his musical career is enough to grant him the legendary status he has achieved.

In this book, you will learn about the man who has released thirty-five albums—nine gold and twenty-five platinum. Willing to work with anyone he thinks is musically talented, Elton

One of Elton John's most recent (and most controversial) collaborations was with rapper Eminem.

John has collaborated, or worked with, some of the greatest and most popular musicians of all time, such as Billy Joel, Aretha Franklin, Stevie Wonder, and John Lennon. At the 2001 Grammy Awards, he startled the world by performing with Eminem, currently one of the most controversial musicians. Elton is often compared to Frank Sinatra because even past his fiftieth birthday he is still one of the most popular musicians in the world.

Elton John is known best, however, for his live performances. They are exciting, strange, and incredibly lively. In fact, he got his big break because of one. In 1971, while playing at the Troubadour in Los Angeles, California, he kicked back his piano bench and began to passionately play his song "Burn Down the Mission" as he stood and wildly danced around his piano. At his first show in America, Elton took the audience and his reviewers by complete surprise and earned himself excellent reviews. Everyone wanted to see him because the audience never knew exactly who he might be or what he might do next. During one show, he might appear on stage and perform dressed as Donald Duck or Minnie Mouse. Other times he wore outrageous glasses while playing. His collection of eyewear has cost him an astounding $40,000.

Yet Elton John has done much more than just perform on stage. In 1994, he and Tim Rice worked together on "Circle of Life" and other music for the movie *The Lion King*. The intensely emotional and melodic soundtrack was number one in the world in 1994. Elton's induction into the Rock and Roll Hall of Fame came that year as well. Elton John has also composed music for the Broadway musical *Aida*, based on an opera by Verdi. It won four Tony Awards, the highest awards in musical theater.

You might wonder how one person could accomplish all of this in just one lifetime. But there's more. In 1992, Elton also became the founder of the most successful charity any entertainer has ever established. Touched by the tragic stories of AIDS and the many friends he had lost to the disease, he began the Elton John AIDS Foundation in the United States and England. To date, the foundation has raised and given away nearly $22 million in grants for education, medical care, and research for HIV and AIDS.

Behind all of these accomplishments there is also a person with an interesting personal story. As you may guess from his accomplishments, Elton's life has held many triumphs, but he

At the funeral of his close friend Diana, the Princess of Wales, Elton John played a special version of his hit "Candle in the Wind."

has also gone through a great deal of struggle and tragedy. For many years, he dealt with the problems of the rocker lifestyle—partying too hard and too often. In fact, Elton often refers to 1989 as the worst year of his life and compares the time to Elvis Presley's depression and fatal drug problems. However, it was not until the mid-1990s that Elton entered drug rehab and cleaned up his life, too late to fix the many regrettable decisions that evolved from his drug use.

Soon after his fiftieth birthday, his life was rocked by the death of two dear friends. A longtime friend of fashion designer Gianni Versace, Elton suffered enormously when Versace was gunned down outside his home in July 1997. The murder was a shock to the world, and Elton's close companion Diana, Princess of Wales, comforted him through his pain. Yet only a month later in August, Diana was killed in an automobile accident in Paris, France. Again the world was horrified and, once again, Elton experienced a tragic and personal loss. To cope with the grief of her death, Elton adapted his hit song "Candle in the Wind," once a tribute to Marilyn Monroe, into "England's Rose." He performed it at Princess Diana's funeral and vowed never to publicly perform the song again.

Presently, Elton John has moved on from this pain-filled time and his life has grown in many different ways. The following chapters will tell you in detail about the life of Elton John, from young boy to legendary rock star.

Born to Rock

Pinner, England, is a small town that lies many miles away from the stylish and hip city of London. There are no tall buildings or busy avenues in Pinner, just two-story homes sitting on quiet, tree-lined streets. On March 25, 1947, one of these homes in Middlesex County, 55 Pinner Hill Road, welcomed Reginald Kenneth Dwight into the world. The proud grandparents (in whose house the baby was born) and the parents could not have known that this child would later become Elton Hercules John—a famous rock star. Instead, Sheila Dwight was happy that her baby boy was born healthy. The baby's father, Stanley Dwight, was absent for his son's birth because he was overseas serving time in England's Royal Air Force (RAF).

Reginald Finds His Passion

With his father away, Reginald spent the earliest years of his life with his mother. They would spend long days at home together as Reginald played. Many times, while his mother was cleaning, she would sit him up on the piano bench in the living room so he could bang on the keys. In interviews now, Sheila always tells her favorite family legend about how one day while she was cleaning she heard Reginald begin to pick out the melody of the song "Skater's Waltz." That's a huge accomplishment for a child, yet Reginald had been listening to his mother's records since the day he was born. Sheila Dwight made sure her son was surrounded by music because she also had a great passion for it.

When Reginald was four, he was sent to the local primary school in Pinner, called Pinner Wood Junior and Mixed Infants. But only a year later his mother pulled him from that school and enrolled him in the Reddiford School. Reddiford was a small private school located in the garden of a teacher named Mr. White. He and his sister personally taught the 100 pupils who went to the school. When Reginald changed schools, his mother also signed him up for piano lessons from a woman who lived in Pinner whose husband was an accomplished musician.

Reggie's talent was immediately seen. He could pick up on notes much faster than most children. Also, unlike many children who dread going off to piano lessons, playing piano was one of Reggie's favorite things to do. He could not wait for his weekly lesson, and at home he spent hours in the living room playing with the keys and making up songs. Though he was not quite a musical prodigy—a child who can play an instrument with little or no instruction—he was certainly incredibly gifted.

A Performer Already

It seems natural that at school Reggie took on the role of performer. He would arrive in the morning with a briefcase full of sheet music— single sheets of paper printed on one or both sides with a song's notes—and quietly take his seat. Sometimes, though, he played piano during the morning assembly and soon he was asked to perform at school concerts and open days, events when parents would come visit the school. These were exciting moments for Reggie because he loved playing and he especially loved playing for other people.

At home Reggie was also the performer. When he was only seven years old, he went to a family member's wedding and, when the band was late to arrive, Reggie walked over to the piano and began to play. He played song after song until the band arrived. Moments like this happened frequently because Reginald simply loved playing the piano.

A Rocky Marriage

By the time Reggie was seven, his parents' marriage was beginning to fall apart. His father, Stanley, was rarely home because he had been promoted to squadron leader, which meant that he traveled most of the time. During the brief times Stanley was home, he did not actively participate in Reggie's life. Rather, Stanley was very quiet and withdrawn, rarely talking to Reggie or Sheila. In fact, even now Elton John regrets not having a close relationship with his father.

In effect, Reggie and his mother turned to one another for companionship. She was his biggest fan. They spent countless hours listening to the radio and practicing the piano. She would sit with him on the bench and cheer him on as he learned a new song. Even now, their relationship is one that they both cherish.

When Reggie was not practicing the piano, he was listening to the radio or watching television. During the mid-1950s, television

Elton John has gained a reputation for putting on incredible live performances in outlandish costumes, such as this one in 1986.

boomed with great pianists, like Joe "Mr. Piano" Henderson and Russ Conway. But Reggie's favorite pianist was Liberace, from America. Liberace was known for his gaudiness, being flashy, colorful, and extravagantly dressed, and Elton John would later credit Liberace for his own outlandish flair.

Royal Academy of Music Sees Talent

In September 1958, at the age of eleven, Reggie left the Reddiford School and started at the local school, Pinner County Grammar School. Luckily, the school's music program was first-rate. The school not only had a grand piano, but the music teacher, Mr. Westgate Smith, was a classical pianist.

Soon after arriving at his new school, Reggie auditioned at the Royal Academy of Music—a school dedicated to teaching gifted children to play music—for possible enrollment as a junior exhibitioner. The junior exhibitioner position would pay for half of Reggie's tuition at the school. Not only did Reggie get accepted, he received a full scholarship to the school—a rarity for a student of his young age.

Helen Piena became Reggie's teacher, and she worked with him every Saturday morning. The first thing the teacher noticed was his ability to play

Did You Know?

Though Elton and his father were anything but close, they did share the common love of soccer, or football as it's called in the United Kingdom. All of the Dwights were actually very fond of the sport. Their favorite team was Pinner's local club, Watford.

In later years, once Elton John had reached the peak of his career, he bought the team. During his brief retirement from performing in 1977, the only time he went in public was to watch his favorite team play football.

Elton John *(right)*, an avid soccer fan and team owner, kicks a soccer ball around with English player George Best in 1976.

music by ear. This means she would play a song and Reggie, without even looking at the sheet music, could play the whole song back to her. This is a remarkable ability and one that few people actually have.

For the next four years, Reggie attended the Royal Academy of Music and learned to fine-tune his gift to play the piano.

Divorce Brings Stronger Devotion to Music

In 1962, Stanley and Sheila Dwight divorced after many years of estrangement, or separation. The divorce meant that Reggie and his mother had to move from his childhood home on Potter Street to an apartment building called Frome Court. This period of Reggie's life was a tough one. He had to adjust to a new home and his mother's new boyfriend. Plus, the move meant he had to leave his friends behind. Though his parents' divorce was not a huge surprise to Reggie, it still made him feel upset, angry, and frustrated. His whole life was uprooted and changed, and although Reggie had known for a long time that his parents were unhappy, he still mourned the loss of their marriage.

Reggie had never been a social butterfly, but now most of his time was spent alone in his bedroom listening to records. He was in love with the Beatles, a four-man band from

23

Liverpool, England. The Beatles were made up of Paul McCartney, John Lennon, George Harrison, and Ringo Starr, and Reggie would listen to their music endlessly in awe of their magnificent rock and roll beats. Reggie also liked a singer named Dusty Springfield—a deep-voiced gospel-like singer. Like Liberace, she was known for her flashy clothes and eyes that were always heavily made up with black eyeliner. Pictures of Dusty Springfield covered his bedroom walls like wallpaper.

As Reggie began to heal from his parents' divorce, he became a little more social at school than he had been before, at least musically. Two of Reggie's greatest traits in the eyes of his classmates were his sense of humor and his great ability to mimic. He could mimic anyone's voice, whether female or male, at any octave (the highness or lowness of a person's voice). Reggie also began to give more lively concerts in the assembly hall of the school. Much to his peers' amazement, Reggie could play the piano like Jerry Lee Lewis, a popular musician at the time.

While playing, he would suddenly jump straight up in the middle of the song, kick back the piano bench, and dance around. His classmates loved it, and they would cheer him on as he entertained them with "Great Balls of Fire"(one of Lewis's hits) at

One of Elton John's heroes, Jerry Lee Lewis, was the inspiration for his piano dance performances.

school concerts, socials, and dances.

Reggie Picks Rock and Roll over Classical Music

Over the next few years, Reggie became more and more engrossed in rock and roll. As a result, he became very unresponsive during his lessons

The Corvettes: Reggie's First Band

During Reggie's fourth year at Pinner County Grammar, he began playing music with a local amateur group called the Corvettes. At the time, Reggie was only fourteen years old. The group played a mix of rock and roll and blues. The founders of the group were two local boys, Stuart Brown and Geoff Dyson, who played guitar and bass. Mick Inkpen played the drums for the band. Mick's father ran a small bar called the Gate, which was very close to where Reggie lived.

Reggie of course played the piano for the band. Unfortunately, though, since pianos cannot be moved around without a lot of help, Reggie always had to play whatever piano was in the bar, no matter how old or new. Most of the time, the piano was horribly out of tune, so the band would actually tune their instruments to the piano, meaning they were making their guitars out of tune! However, it was a smart move because their songs ended up sounding much better than if the piano was out of tune and the other instruments were in tune.

The Corvettes broke up after only a few performances. Each member went his own way, but six months later they met up and decided to try playing together again. With a new name, Bluesology, they began relying on Geoff Dyson, the bass player, as their booking manager— the person who finds the band gigs to play. At the time, none of them knew that Bluesology would not only stay together but play with some of the biggest names in rock and roll.

at the Royal Academy of Music. Once a motivated student, Reggie started to skip classes until he did not even bother to show up on Saturday mornings. At fifteen, classical instruction no longer appealed to him. Now, his passion was all wrapped up in the jolting music of rock and roll. His new stepfather, Fred Farebrother, worked hard to encourage Reggie in his musical pursuits. He was actually the person who got Reggie his first audition to be the pianist at the pub in the Northwood Hills Hotel. Reggie got the gig.

For his first public show, Reggie dressed in his best tweed jacket and was escorted by his mother and stepfather. The crowd was anything but welcoming during the performance. Some screamed "Get off the stage!" while others threw ashtrays at the boy playing songs by Ray Charles, Jim Reeves, and the Beatles. But Reggie stayed onstage and played more songs. He even finished his performance in good humor, all the while knowing the audience openly disliked his music. For the next two years, Reggie played every Saturday night at

Northwood Hills, and as time passed his popularity grew. By no means was he ever a raving sensation at the pub, but after a while, Reggie had crowds that enjoyed listening to him play.

Reggie Drops Out of School

During the mid-1960s in Middlesex, England, a musical career was viewed as a dream that would never become reality. No one from Middlesex had ever become famous, and Reggie's teachers did not envision him breaking the mold. Rather, they saw a young boy who rarely paid attention. In 1965, when Reggie met with career advisers to talk about his future, they also did not see a rock star. They saw a student with failing grades.

The eighteen-year-old Reggie decided to leave school to pursue his musical career. This risky decision could have ruined his chances for success. But Reggie, in this case, got lucky. Although he denied himself an education, he still achieved his dreams.

29

1947
Reginald Kenneth Dwight is born on March 25 in Pinner, Middlesex, England.

1961
Reginald joins a local R & B band, the Corvettes.

1967
Reginald changes his name to Elton John and meets Bernie Taupin, an unknown writer from Lincolnshire, who would write Elton's lyrics for the next thirty-plus years.

1969
Elton releases his first album, *Empty Sky*, in the UK and the album gains him a small following.

1970
In August, Elton John makes his name as a lively performer at a Los Angeles concert when he jumps up and plays his song "Burn Down the Mission" while standing up and dancing.

1974
Elton releases his first hits compilation, simply called *Greatest Hits*. In later years it becomes the biggest seller of all the Elton John albums.

1990
Elton establishes the Elton John AIDS Foundation, the most successful charity ever created by an entertainer.

1998
On February 24, Elton John receives a knighthood for his contribution to music and his AIDS fund-raising.

1977
In November, Elton announces he is retiring from performing and isolates himself inside his three mansions.

1994
Elton John is inducted into the Rock and Roll Hall of Fame.

1997
Elton experiences profound loss when his friends Gianni Versace and Princess Diana both die unexpectedly.

Success Comes Slowly

After dropping out of school, Reggie concentrated only on his career. He took a job with a music company on Denmark Street. Denmark Street in London housed most of the music industry's publishers. Reggie's job was with Mills Music, an American firm whose clients included some very famous people, such as

Fats Waller, Duke Ellington, and Leroy Anderson. Reggie didn't interact with the performers but instead worked in the warehouse, filling orders, packing boxes with sheet music, and preparing tea for his boss. The job was not glamorous or fulfilling, but it made Reggie feel like he was part of the music world, a feeling he truly loved.

Bluesology Gets a Manager and a Record Deal

While Reggie was working at Mills Music, he did not stop playing with his band, Bluesology. The band still had four members: Reg (no longer Reggie to anyone but his mother) on piano, Stuart Brown on guitar and vocals, Mick Inkpen on drums, and Rex Bishop on bass. They met every Saturday and practiced in the back of the Northwood Hills Hotel. They entered contests and played at dances throughout the area, but it was not until they got a band manager that things began to pick up.

Mick worked at a jewelry store, and for months he had been bothering his boss, Arnold

Tendler, to come see Bluesology play. Finally, Arnold agreed to see one performance. He was impressed by what he saw, especially Reg's playing. He found it fascinating when Reg kicked back his bench and played the piano sitting on the floor. Arnold gave the band money to buy new instruments, and he also financed a two-sided demo tape at a studio in Rickmansworth, England.

Once the tape was completed, Arnold made the rounds to record companies armed with Bluesology's tape. He went door-to-door, day after day, and at each office he received a polite but firm no. However, Arnold finally met with success when he interviewed with Jack Baverstock of Philips Records. Philips Records was a middle-sized music company with a lot of young talent. Jack agreed to sign the band to Fontana, a smaller label associated with Philips.

The band was ecstatic about the news. They were signed! People were willing to pay them to make music. All those nights in smelly bars with inattentive audiences had finally paid off. They were going to be rock stars.

Making It Big?

On June 3, 1965, Bluesology recorded their record, featuring Reg's original song "Come Back, Baby." Only a few months later, the song was released and the band heard it played on the radio. Even though it only played for a few weeks before failing ever to appear again, the band had been removed from amateur status. They no longer had to settle for playing at local dances. They could now set their sights on larger, more serious venues, like the Last Chance and the 100 Club—two very cool clubs in London.

On July 22, Bluesology received another big boost to their musical careers: their first write-up. *Record Retailer and Music Industry News* was a trade magazine, a magazine that concentrates on one area of interest, such as music. They wrote about Bluesology in a positive light and quoted Mick Inkpen about their style of music.

Bluesology Adds a New Section

Toward the end of 1965, Pat Higgs, a semiprofessional trumpeter, read in a trade publication that an up-and-coming band was looking to add a bass section. Auditions were being held in Middlesex, England. Both Pat and a man named Dave Murphy, a tenor saxophonist, made it to auditions that day and both were welcomed into Bluesology.

Their first major performance was at a band contest at a place called the

Fun Fact!

If Bluesology was not making it on the charts in June 1965, who was? The radio blared that summer with the Rolling Stones' "Satisfaction," the Byrds' "Mr. Tambourine Man," and the Kinks' "Set Me Free."

State, a large cinema modeled to look like the Empire State Building. After they played three songs, the band was approached by a representative of the Roy Tempest Agency. He wanted to know if the band would be interested in backing American rhythm and blues (R & B) singers on tour in Britain. Basically, he was offering the band the opportunity to go on the road. The band's answer was an enthusiastic yes!

Reg quit his job at Mills Music the next day. At the age of eighteen, Elton John's long road to fame took its first small steps.

On the Road

The first major performer to hire Bluesology was Major Lance, a well-known blues singer whose most remembered song is "Um Um Um Um Um Um." Reg knew the words by heart because he had listened to Major Lance for years. This was an important moment in the life of Elton John because not only did he get to meet an idol, but Elton got to perform with him as well. Reg's dreams were coming true, and as the weeks rolled by this happened more and more. The band started playing for big names like the Drifters, the Ink Spots, Billy Stewart, Doris Troy, and Patti LaBelle.

While on tour playing for other musicians, the band still played on its own, and in February 1966, Bluesology released another song on the Fontana label. This song, "Mr. Frantic," was also written by Reg. Again, though, the song was not played on the radio more than a few times.

Major Changes Within Bluesology

The lack of success hit Reg really hard, and he started to become frustrated and put less energy into the band. He felt guilty for not producing hits, and he moved into the background when the band played, not really caring about his performance. One night while they were playing at a rather well-known venue called the Cromwellian Club in South Kensington, London, Long John Baldry dropped in. Long John was a very successful singer signed to the same label as the Rolling Stones. He offered Bluesology a job playing backup for his band. Though Bluesology were still under contract with Arnold Tendler, they immediately took the job.

The band thought touring with Long John would be a great move for them. However, the group's dynamic was radically changed when they began the tour. To begin with, Mick and Rex were replaced by Pete Gavin and Freddy Gandy. Neil Hubbard took over for Stuart Brown on guitar and became a backup vocalist rather than the lead singer. The horn section was completely revamped as Marc Charig became the trumpeter and Elton Dean became the tenor sax player. For Reg, playing with Long John also meant he would not be singing anymore. This setup caused intense frustration for him. It disappointed him so much that he began to think about getting out of performing and going back to office work.

Hope from Liberty

While touring with Bluesology, Reg saw a poster announcing that Liberty Records was looking for new talent. At the time, Reg was fighting

Elton sits with record industry executives backstage in 1970. By then, he had started to make it big in the music business.

depression and feeling especially unhappy about his current musical path. But Reg decided to give this audition everything he had.

Weeks later, when Reg sat in the office of Ray Williams, the scout for new talent at Liberty Records, all of Bluesology's upbeat material flew out of his head. Instead, Reg began to play slower, sadder music that matched and vented all of his current dissatisfaction, like Jim Reeves's "He'll Have to Go." Though Ray Williams knew the young man sitting at the piano was not what one would call "hip," he could not help but be impressed with his ability to play piano and sing. There was something about Reg that Ray simply liked. Perhaps it was intuition or fate, but Ray Williams suggested that Reg make a demo tape to take to his boss at Liberty Records.

Sitting with Ray, Reg admitted right away that he did not write lyrics very well. Indeed, he was pretty bad at them; however, Reg loved writing the music. Somewhere in the back of Ray Williams's mind he remembered a letter he had received a few months before from a man named Bernard Taupin. Bernard had expressed the

Bernard Taupin: Poetry Makes Music

Bernard Taupin was raised in Lincolnshire, England, and early on fell in love with the written word. As a young boy, he read anything he could get his hands on, from *Winnie-the-Pooh* to *The Chronicles of Narnia* by C. S. Lewis. He soon graduated to writing stories himself. Though Bernie loved writing, he never thought he would pursue a writing career until one night he heard Bob Dylan's "The Times They Are A-Changin'" on his father's radio. The next day he quit his factory job and began to write musical lyrics.

exact opposite of Reg's problem: He could write great lyrics but could not compose music. He made a mental note to contact Bernard in Lincolnshire, England, so the two could meet.

By the time the letter from Liberty Records arrived at Bernie Taupin's home, he had seen so many dead ends with his music he was not immediately excited. Even though the

Elton John circa 1977 in Paris, France, around the time of his announced retirement

record company wanted an interview, Bernie had received many letters like this one. He set it aside and decided he would go see Ray Williams in a few months.

Meanwhile, Reg was again pessimistic about his whole career, feeling lost and unhopeful. In the beginning, Ray Williams had seemed promising, but things appeared to be going downhill fast. Reg also felt another blow when Ray said his bosses had listened to Reg's demo tape and were not impressed. However, Ray explained to Reg that he thought they were wrong. Ray then introduced Reg to Nick James, Kirk Duncan, members of the band the Hollies, and Dick James of Dick James Music (DJM). The Hollies, named after the singer Buddy Holly, had been trying to break into the music scene since the beginning of the1960s. They had established more connections with important people than Reg had. Their music was also considered innovative like Reg's, so they were helpful to bounce ideas off of and work with.

Elton John takes a breather backstage with members of his band.

Success Begins to Brew

Dick James was a big man in the music business, having helped many musicians record and release their albums at his studio at 71–75 New Oxford Street. Reg was introduced to Dick James during the summer of 1967, and within a few days he was meeting and hanging out with all of his idols, like Graham Nash and Allan Clarke of the Hollies, and Roger Greenway. Then, with only a few weeks of the summer left, Bernie Taupin came to town for his interview with Ray Williams.

As soon as Ray showed Bernie's lyrics to Reg, Reg liked them. And when the pair began to work together, their ability to make good music was apparent to everyone. Their first piece together was called "Scarecrow," and everyone who listened to it was drawn to its melody and emotion.

Bernie and Reg worked well together because their talents blended perfectly. Bernie could write amazing lyrics, and Reg could write marvelous music. Strangely enough, the two men rarely worked together in the same room. Instead, Bernie would send the lyrics to Reg in the mail. Reg would receive them at the studio on New Oxford Street or on the road with Bluesology, and working late into the night he would put music to the lyrics. Now all Bernie and Reg needed was a chance.

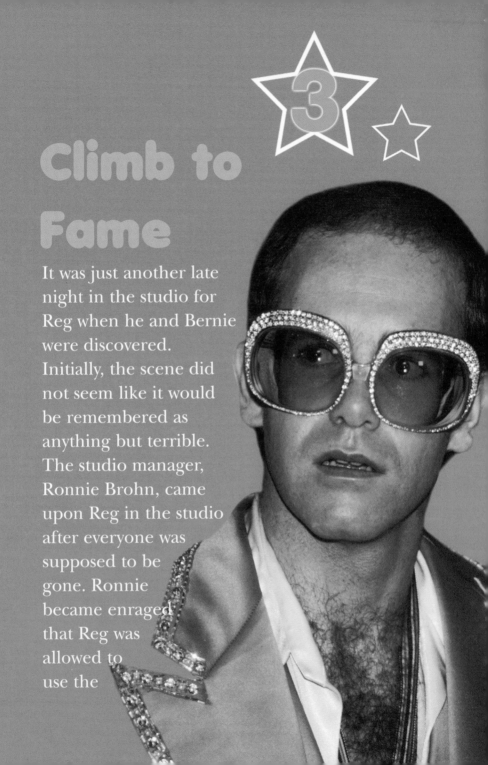

Climb to Fame

It was just another late night in the studio for Reg when he and Bernie were discovered. Initially, the scene did not seem like it would be remembered as anything but terrible. The studio manager, Ronnie Brohn, came upon Reg in the studio after everyone was supposed to be gone. Ronnie became enraged that Reg was allowed to use the studio after hours. The next day Ronnie went to Stephen James, the day manager, and told him that Caleb Quaye, who worked at the studio, was allowing Reg to use the studio's resources without authority. Stephen James looked at the problem another way. He wondered why a musician was allowed to use the studio and not share his work.

When Stephen asked Caleb why Reg and Bernie did not allow others to listen to their music, Caleb told him it was because the two-man team was not very good. Stephen asked to hear the music anyway, and when he listened, he completely disagreed with Caleb. He thought their music was interesting; it was something new. He took the tape to his father, Dick James, the next day.

The Moment It Turned

Dick James worked with the Beatles, and by the summer of 1967, Beatlemania was at its highest peak. The world was awash with love for the songs "Lucy in the Sky with Diamonds" and "All You Need Is Love." Teenagers everywhere knew every single word to their songs. Public appearances were out-of-control episodes. No teenager could get enough of the Beatles, and Dick James was their music publisher. He handled the copyrights to their songs and helped them get exposure. So, when Dick James called Reg and Bernie into his office, they didn't know what to expect. They had no idea that Dick James was about to offer them the opportunity of a lifetime. He offered to put Reg and Bernie under contract as songwriters for Dick James Music.

The two were ecstatic. Reg had been looking and hoping to escape Bluesology, and Bernie had just been looking for someone to see something in his work. Both were overwhelmed with hope for their careers.

Becoming Elton John

On November 7, 1967, Reg and Bernie signed with Dick James Music. However, since both boys were not yet twenty-one, their parents had to be there to witness the signing. Initially, the contract was only for the two musicians to write songs, not perform them. However, as Dick James took the demo tape of the songs around, more and more music executives remarked on Reg's talent.

Only a few months later, Dick offered Reg another deal. This time he wanted to put Reg under contract to record his own music, with lyrics written by Bernie. Again Reg accepted, and soon he was working on producing new songs.

A few nights after Dick offered Reg the record deal, Reg played his last gig with Bluesology. After their first set, Reg approached his band mate Elton Dean and asked a favor of him. He wanted to use Elton's name, but Dean thought that was a lot to ask, so Reg suggested "Elton John." Elton Dean had no problem with this. That night Reg Dwight became Elton John, and soon the world would know his name.

Heading in the Right Direction

The first Elton John single, "I've Been Loving You," was released in March 1968, the same month as his birthday. The song was a simple ballad written by Stephen James, although

Bernie was given full credit as the writer. The song never made it anywhere that summer and it slipped onto dusty shelves like so many unknown artists' work. However, Dick persuaded Elton to put together another demo tape, which got good reviews from music executives around town.

In September 1968, Steven Brown joined DJM. Upon his arrival, it was decided he would be the producer for Bernie and Elton. When Steven heard their newest creation, "Lady Samantha," a song about a sad medieval woman, he was so impressed he decided the song should be released. After months in the studio, "Lady Samantha" was released on January 10, 1969. Though the song never made it onto the charts, it got the attention of the right people. Trade magazines likes the *New Musical Express, Disco, Music Echo, Melody Maker,* and *Michelin* all gave the song rave reviews.

Empty Sky Is Released in London

In February 1969, Elton and Bernie put together their first record, called *Empty Sky*. It was released soon after with full-blown advertising to fuel interest in the new artist Elton John. Splayed across the sides of buses in London was a sign that read "Elton John" with colored circles bordering its edges.

The record itself was full of whimsical, emotional songs. "Empty Sky" was about a

Who Did Elton John Listen to in 1971?

You might imagine that someone who plays music would listen to a lot of it. Elton John has confessed that he loves it all. When asked in 1971 what kind of music he listened to, he said, "Pretty much everything, aside from easy listening and traditional jazz . . . I like the stuff Miles [Davis] has put out, and Charles Lloyd and Chick Corea and some of the stuff Sun Ra does—and I like the Band and Neil Young, and Burt Bacharach is a genius."

Perhaps Elton does not enjoy easy listening because for a while he was supporting himself by recording Muzak for supermarkets!

prisoner unhappy with his lost freedom; "Western Gateway" celebrated the American frontier; "Gulliver" was about one of Bernie's old pets. All of the songs shared a heartfelt theme and one that not many people found subtle. In the end, the album sold only 4,000 copies in the United Kingdom—an amount not considered successful. Overall, the album was a commercial flop.

A New Album: *Elton John*

After the unsuccessful release of *Empty Sky*, Steven Brown pushed Elton to make a new album. On March 6, 1970, the album *Elton John* was launched at one of London's coolest clubs, the Revolution. Though the album ran over its budget by $5,000, the end result was worth it—people liked it and were buying it. Within a few months, it was on Britain's Top 50 while worldwide it was ranked number eleven. Overall, 10,000 copies were sold, which was enormous progress in comparison to *Empty Sky*.

Even in the studio, those working on the project knew it was going to mean something.

Gus Dudgeon produced *Elton John,* and in an interview with *Billboard* magazine in 1997, he related his feelings as the album was being produced: "He [Elton] saw himself as a songwriter. I was primarily commissioned to do the Elton John album as sort of a glamorous demo. We cut the album in a week, and I never stopped grinning from beginning to end because it all fell into place so brilliantly."

Dick James realized soon after the album's completion that it was time for Elton to get a band manager and go on tour. He wanted the world to know Elton John.

On Tour, Playing at the Troubadour

Many music lovers in America are picky; they like well-known groups, and new talent is often ignored. Located in Los Angeles, the Troubadour was considered one of the hardest venues to succeed in. On August 25, 1970, Elton John was racked with nervousness as he waited to take the Troubadour's stage. The crowd was large and tough, and he knew he was going to have to play his absolute best.

When Elton went on stage, the audience did not roar with applause; in fact most of the people kept talking. Halfway through his third song, with the audience chattering, Elton's anger got the best of him. He stood up suddenly and screamed, "Right! If you won't listen, perhaps you'll bloody well listen to this." As he yelled, he kicked back his piano bench and started playing his song "Burn Down the Mission" on the piano like Jerry Lee Lewis. He was excited with anger. His music came alive. He danced and sang. The audience had no idea what to do, so they responded. They whooped and cheered, screaming along to the music even though they did not know a single word. The show was an awesome hit, and afterward so many fans wanted to meet Elton that a friend had to act as a bodyguard. The next day the critics wrote up glowing reviews.

The *Los Angeles Times* ran a story with the headline "Elton John: New Rock Talent." The opening sentence was a single word: "Rejoice." Elton had achieved a lot in just one night. He had hurdled over the challenge of reaching an audience that was notoriously hard to reach. In fact, they loved him. Suddenly, he was no longer climbing to the top. Elton John had arrived.

Tumbleweed Connection and More Touring

In August 1970, Elton's third album, *Tumbleweed Connection*, was released. This album celebrated

Did You Know?

"Your Song," from *Elton John*, was a number that Bernie wrote in fifteen minutes at Elton's mother's breakfast table in Frome Court. The song, released in January 1971, hit the world and rocked listeners. Within only a week of its release, it was number seven on Britain's charts and simultaneously brought Elton John into the American top ten. "Your Song" is actually Elton and Bernie's most popular song to date, as famous as the incredibly popular Beatles' song "Yesterday."

Elton John crafted a flamboyant image that he started employing while on tour in the United States in 1970.

Bernie's deep love for the Old West. As a child, he was hooked on tales of Billy the Kid and the Oregon Trail. The mood of the album was folkie and down-home, with references to trains, riverboats, preachers, and cornfields. Song titles on the album included "My Father's Gun," "Ballad of a Well-Known Gun," and the infamous "Burn Down the Mission" from his passionate performance at the Troubadour only a few months before. Within just a few weeks, the album reached an amazing number five on the *Billboard* magazine charts.

After a short break, Elton went back on the road to make more American fans. Pictures started popping up from America of Elton on tour in strange outfits and dramatic stage costumes. One photo in *Rolling Stone* magazine was taken by a young photographer named Annie Liebowitz—a woman who is now famous for her work. In this picture, Elton is onstage dressed in red underwear, with socks pulled up to his knees and a pair of boots. His mouth is wide open and his fists are clenched. Elton knew that America demanded spectacular stars,

and since he did not look like a star, he would make up for it by acting and dressing like one. He decided he would be fantastic and eccentric—pure star qualities.

Elton's offstage personality, however, was just as down-to-earth and quiet as ever. He still lived with his

Elton John blows a kiss to the audience at the Forum in Los Angeles in 1974.

mother in Frome Court. Many interviewers also commented on how strange it was to watch his lively concerts and then go backstage to interview him and find the vivacious performer gone. In front of them sat a quiet, shy young man.

Elton was so shy that he even had trouble approaching other performers. One night while playing at the Fillmore East in

Philadelphia, Pennsylvania, Elton went to
Bernie backstage and very quietly told him to
follow him. Bernie thought it was something
serious so he stopped working and followed
Elton through the maze of people backstage.
When they stopped, Elton introduced Bernie to
Bob Dylan, an idol of both of theirs. Elton
looked at Bernie after introducing him to Bob
Dylan and just beamed.

Top of the Charts

In the early 1970s, the record-buying public began expanding their musical interests. They started to look more to solo artists for inspiring music. Though the majority still loved the Beatles and the Rolling Stones, some of the most popular performers also included Cat Stevens, Gilbert O'Sullivan, and, of course, Bob Dylan.

Elton John exploded onto the music scene at a time when rock and roll was growing. Popularity was no longer restricted to groups with young, good-looking men. Now the people making popular music had more meaningful qualities—talent, vitality, and the ability to make good music.

11-17-70 and *Friends*

Elton released his fourth and fifth albums right after one another. In April 1971, *11-17-70* was released to the public, and in May, *Friends* was also released. Both albums soared in popularity, selling out in America and England. *Friends* went gold only two months after its release—a huge accomplishment for Elton.

While the albums climbed the charts, Elton was on the road again doing a fifty-five-city tour of America. It was this tour that brought Elton to the million-dollar mark. But even with his newfound success, Elton was still as quiet as ever offstage. Many interviewers found it perplexing and began to report it in the press. Articles spoke of a quiet, polite young man who seemed to not understand the extent of his accomplishments. The reports were true, though. The speed with which fame came for Elton made it hard for him to grasp his popularity. Another factor was the simple fact that he was still so young—only twenty-four years old. Only the year before he had been living with his mother back in Frome Court. Now he sat atop the complex world of success.

Madman Across the Water

Elton's sixth album came out in November 1971. Only a few months earlier, Elton had been soaring to the top. However, musicians who shoot to the top so quickly have a tendency to fizzle out fast. The words "passé" and "fad" began to pop up in articles written about Elton. The word "struggling" began to appear next. The media is a tough yet vital aspect of a musician's career, however. The media holds so much influence that it can make or break a musician. Looking for a story, the media began to try to break Elton, but he would have none of it. *Madman Across the Water* was Elton's attempt to deflect the negative reports.

The album was an intense experience for both Bernie and Elton. Before, such as on *Tumbleweed Connection*, the two had been dreaming about an America they had never even seen. Now they had spent a better part of a year on the road in America, and their perception of the country had changed because of it. Their music was also affected.

All of the songs on the album were about tour life. "Tiny Dancer" was a love song for Bernie's wife, Maxine. "Holiday Inn" was about the endless flights and similar hotel rooms they stayed in each night while on tour. Finally, in "All the Nasties," Bernie and Elton wrote to all of the music critics who had been taking swipes at them all year. The album was considered brilliant in the United States, making it to number eight on the American *Billboard* chart. Britain, however, was another story, as the album was not as well received. In truth, it barely even made a splash— a fact that was very unsettling for Elton. He had hoped it would knock them senseless. But

Elton John struts his stuff for the crowd in Earls Court in London, England, during a 1976 concert.

there were positive things going on in America. Aside from the Beatles, Elton was the only other musician to have four albums in the American top ten simultaneously. This was a huge success, and it helped Elton cope with his lack of success in Britain, his homeland.

Honky Chateau

In early 1972, Elton arranged with the Rolling Stones to use their elaborate and very chic recording studio. Located in the French Riviera, the studio was top-notch. However, only a few days before Elton and his crew were scheduled to depart for the studio, word came that it was no longer available. The Rolling Stones were known for being unreliable, and a new place had to be found quickly. Staying with the inviting idea of recording in France, a new studio named Strawberry was found. The studio was located in the Chateau d'Herouville.

Established in the seventeenth century, Chateau d'Herouville was set in the countryside of France, only thirty miles outside of Paris. It was a place already known to great bands; Jerry Garcia and the Grateful Dead had recorded there only a few months earlier. Elton flew over right away to have a look at the place, and he fell in love with it instantly. He loved that he could record in a room with three chandeliers. Each room also had huge windows that looked out over miles of rolling vineyards.

Fun Fact!

On December 8, 1971, Elton John became legal. No, he did not turn twenty-one. Rather, he legally changed his name to Elton Hercules John. The name "Elton" was borrowed from his friend, Elton Dean. "John" was taken from his old boss, Long John Baldry. And "Hercules" came from a character on Elton's favorite television show, *Steptoe and Son*. From that day forward, Reginald Kenneth Dwight was no more.

When the band arrived, a charged energy filled the air. Perhaps it was the beautiful surroundings and the lavish studio. Or maybe it was simply a good time for all of them. Whatever the reason, the songs recorded over the next few weeks would make an enormous impact on Elton's career.

"Rocket Man"

It took only ten weeks to finish all ten songs for the new album, *Honky Chateau,* named for the chateau in which the songs were recorded. One of the songs stood out more than the others, even while it was being recorded. The song was "Rocket Man."

The song's concept was not a completely original idea—David Bowie's 1969 "Space Oddity" had also been about a lonely astronaut. Regardless, the song still contained that unexplainable "thing" that makes a fantastic piece of music. In fact, when released in 1972, the song was the single Elton had been hoping for in the U.K. It quickly went to number two in Britain and number six in America. Amazingly, the song also sparked a second burst of Elton John mania all over the world.

"Rocket Man" also helped *Honky Chateau* do exceptionally well on the charts. Though the rest of the songs had more of a country-western feel, the album made it to number two on every single British chart and number one on every American one. It also went platinum in 1995, because it had sold a million copies. *Honky Chateau* was the first of Elton's seven consecutive number-one albums.

Dominating the Charts

The years 1972 through 1975 were the peak years of Elton John's career. During this time, Elton's music was heard by huge numbers of adoring fans. In fact, between 1972 and 1975, Elton had seven consecutive number-one albums. In 1973, *Don't Shoot Me, I'm Only the Piano Player*, and *Goodbye Yellow Brick Road* were released, followed by *Caribou* in 1974, and Elton began to dominate the charts. In 1973, "Crocodile Rock" was his first number-one hit. That same year, "Daniel" and

"Goodbye Yellow Brick Road" reached number two on the charts. Then came a tremendous wave of success in 1974 and 1975 on the American *Billboard* charts:

- "Bennie and the Jets" reached number one.
- "Don't Let the Sun Go Down on Me" reached number two.
- A cover of the Beatles' "Lucy in the Sky with Diamonds" reached number one.
- "Philadelphia Freedom" reached number one.
- "Someone Saved My Life Tonight" reached number four.
- "Island Girl" reached number one.

Also that year, "Captain Fantastic and the Brown Dirt Cowboy," released in April 1975, was his first song ever to debut at number one. Elton received a star on the Hollywood Walk of Fame, and his face graced the cover of *Time* magazine—he was in the middle of superstardom. In a 1974 interview printed in *Melody Maker*, Elton explained how he worked and commented on his new success: "I only play for pleasure when I

Elton John performing on the popular '70s television show *Soul Train*

write. I never sit down and play, but if I do I always try and sing other people's songs. I like doing sessions. I used to do a lot of sessions at one time, and I miss doing them. People won't ring me any more because I'm too busy. I did Rod's [Stewart] and Lennon's things. They were not really sessions, just friends asking me down. And I did a Neil Sedaka and Ringo Starr."

Top of the Charts, but Falling

Two years later, in 1977, Elton had become fully acclimated to the rock-star lifestyle. He was a wealthy big-spender surrounded mostly by famous people, and he loved to party. Unfortunately, many Hollywood parties were and still are known not only for their extravagance but also for the abundance of available drugs.

During the mid '70s, Elton had become a user. Like so many people who try drugs, at first he used them only at parties. Then it was only on weekends. Then, only at night. Soon Elton fell into the cyclical trap of addiction. He would come down and feel so bad all he would

Playing with His Biggest Idol

On Thanksgiving 1975, at Madison Square Garden in New York City, Elton experienced another triumphant achievement.

His concert that night was a stellar engagement made even more splendid by the appearance of John Lennon. As the two grasped each other in a hug after singing "Lucy in the Sky with Diamonds," Elton murmured into his microphone, "This has been a very emotional evening for me." In fact, that evening was one of the most emotional ever for Elton. He had been listening to the Beatles for years, and now he was playing alongside one of his idols.

want was to go back up. So he took more drugs until he found himself using drugs most of the time. His body and mind were quickly affected. His moods sank, and soon his music did, too. Though he was still moving through his life performing and recording music, none of it felt like it mattered to him anymore.

By November 1977, Elton had fallen far—so far, in fact, he announced he was retiring from performing and would only record one album a year. More important, however, he and Bernie Taupin ceased working together, severing a relationship many had once labeled "a hit factory." Bernie headed out to Los Angeles to pursue new interests, and Elton spent the next two years secluded in his three mansions, only making public appearances at the games of the Watford football team that he had bought a few years earlier. However, even with all of the obvious clues and knowledge that drugs change the course of one's life and never for the better, Elton continued to abuse himself. In other words, he kept falling.

Elton was on and off drugs until the mid-1990s when, after years of struggling, he checked himself into a rehabilitation center. Supported by a close friend, Elton finally stopped abusing drugs and chose his own health and happiness.

Rocket Man Falls and Returns

The early 1970s were a blur of superstardom for Elton, and the end of the decade—even with his retirement—was just as jam-packed. He kept himself in the music scene with the release of four albums from 1976 to 1979: *Here and There, Blue Moves, A Single Man*, and *Victim of Love*. *Here and There* and *Blue Moves* sold over two million copies. Elton's 1976 duet with Kiki Dee, "Don't Go Breaking My Heart," also reached the top of the U.K. charts. Then, in 1979, only two years after his retirement from performing, Elton decided to stage a comeback tour and renew his old love for the stage. He kicked off the tour with a free concert in Central Park, located in New York City. When Elton came out on stage, he was dressed as Donald Duck. The world tour was extensive, including shows in the Soviet Union, making Elton the first Westerner to tour that communist land.

Losing John Lennon

Perhaps if tragedy had not struck him so hard, Elton John would have been able to pull himself out of the blackness in which he found himself. However, on the night of December 8, 1980, while entering his New York City apartment building, John Lennon was murdered by Mark Chapman, a crazed fan.

Elton was incredibly close to Lennon. Elton had idolized him as a young man and then befriended him later in life. The two shared a deep passion for music and the world. Elton

Elton jams onstage with Kiki Dee, with whom he released the duet "Don't Go Breaking My Heart."

was the godfather to Lennon and Yoko Ono's only son, Sean. Their bond was strong. On that night, as the world sat stunned facing the tragedy of losing a talented musician like John Lennon, Elton faced life and the world without the companionship of his close friend.

Jump Up!

In 1980, a short time after Bernie and Elton separated, the old team returned to the world of music with the albums *21 at 33* and *The Fox.* After collaborating with other artists and publishing a book of his own poems, called *The One Who Writes the Words for Elton John*, Bernie Taupin was ready to reunite the dynamic duo. Elton, for his part, was refreshed from his long hiatus from music. Both *21 at 33* and *The Fox* did very well on the charts. But Elton's music had changed.

The 1980s had caused Elton to calm down a bit musically and rely less on the pop sound. His music became slower, more mellow, and more bluesy. In reviews, his music was being labeled as adult contemporary, meaning Elton's audience was changing from youth to adulthood.

In 1981, Elton released *Jump Up!*, a new album that included a tribute song to John Lennon, called "Hey Hey Johnny." Elton finally made peace with his friend's death in August 1982, when he performed the song at his sold-out show in Madison Square Garden with Yoko Ono and Sean Lennon. Then, in 1983, Elton made it huge again by reviving the enormous success of the '70s with his release of "I Guess That's Why They Call It the Blues," featuring Stevie Wonder on harmonica. The song made it all the way to number four on the charts, placing Elton back in the popular music category. The song showed that Elton could still produce music everyone loved.

Elton Gets Married

In 1984, on Valentine's Day, Elton surprised the world when he married his short-time girlfriend and studio engineer, Renate Blauel, in a small church in Australia. Perhaps the world would not have been so surprised if not for the sheer fact that everyone had believed Elton was a homosexual, or attracted to people of the same sex. At that point, it had yet to be confirmed by Elton publicly, and it had almost always been suspected for various reasons, mainly due to the fact that he never dated anyone.

Elton's marriage lasted four years but inevitably ended in divorce. Those four years were some of Elton's worst. He was lost, lonely, and did not understand why

Fun Fact!

Even before he could read, Elton could recognize almost every album cover in his mother's collection. Elton would later say that his first memory was looking through his parents' huge collection of records. He gives credit to his mother for his interest in music. "My mother introduced me to rock and roll," he said. "One day she came home with 'ABC Boogie' by Bill Haley, and 'Heartbreak Hotel' by Elvis Presley. She has always been well up on what's going on."

Elton John married Renate Blauel, his studio engineer, on Valentine's Day of 1984.

he did the things he did. These feelings provoked him to take more drugs, and as the '80s wrapped up he was in serious danger, both mentally and physically. Elton compares this period of his life to that of Elvis Presley—a known drug user who later died from the disastrous effects of misusing prescription medication.

Ryan White

Elton was feeling lost, living without hope or direction. He began to look out at the rest of the world to find something meaningful. For Elton, inspiration came from a young boy named Ryan White.

Ryan White was diagnosed as a hemophiliac— a person whose blood does not clot—when he was only three years old. Hemophiliacs are at high risk of death from small injuries, which can cause extensive bleeding that the body cannot stop. Tragically, when Ryan was young, medical science did not understand the AIDS virus, or how it was contracted.

In 1984, after surgery due to complications from pneumonia, Ryan White found out that he had contracted AIDS, a disease that breaks down the body's immune system until it can no longer fight off even small illnesses like the common cold. He was given only a few months to live. However, Ryan was a fighter, and as the months passed his will to live increased. Even while Ryan fought the disease, he also had to fight discrimination. Unfortunately, people were still very uneducated about AIDS, and so Ryan suffered many prejudices. In his hometown, neighbors and kids harassed him and rallied for him to be kicked out of school.

Elton John was well informed of the mounting AIDS crisis across the United States and throughout the world. Ryan's story tugged at his heart and spurred Elton to action. Splitting the bills with Michael Jackson, Elton covered Ryan's medical expenses. Elton was at Ryan's bedside when he died in 1990. He performed at Ryan's funeral and soon after checked himself into a drug and alcohol treatment center. He also announced to the world that he was gay.

The Elton John AIDS Foundation

Music was not the focus of Elton's life during
the late '80s and the first few years of the '90s.
Rather, he was fighting to find his way through
a dark and difficult time in his life. In 1992, one
of the ways Elton found hope was by starting an
AIDS organization. Partly because of his
touching experience with Ryan White, as well as
his sexual orientation, Elton felt his fame could
be used for a meaningful cause.

The Elton John AIDS Foundation, with
offices in England and the United States, was
that cause. With Elton as the chair of the
foundation, the organization provides
educational AIDS-prevention programs and
funds health-care services for AIDS/HIV patients
all over the world. The foundation directs 90
percent of its profits to direct care and 10
percent to AIDS prevention. Elton adds to the
$22 million the foundation dispenses each year
by pledging all of his profits from singles

Elton John

Elton John performed Queen's "Bohemian Rhapsody" in memory of the group's vocalist, Freddie Mercury, who died of AIDS in 1991.

released after "The One" to the foundation. "The One" reached number eight on the charts in 1992.

Elton soon found himself in the fulfilling role of AIDS activist. In 1992, he performed at the Freddie Mercury Memorial and AIDS Benefit concert at Wembley Stadium in England, alongside Axl Rose

And the Award Goes To

Elton John has won eight Grammy Awards during his career:

- **1987: Song of the Year and Pop Vocal Performance by a Duo or Group, "That's What Friends Are For"**
- **1988: Performance in a Music Video, *The Prince's Trust All-Star Rock Concert***
- **1992: Instrumental Composition, "Basque"**
- **1994: Male Pop Vocal Performance, "Can You Feel the Love Tonight"**
- **1997: Male Pop Vocal Performance, "Candle in the Wind 1997"**
- **1998: Musical Show Album, *The Lion King***
- **1999: Grammy Legend Award**

of Guns N' Roses. Freddie Mercury was the lead singer of the band Queen who died from AIDS in 1991. Elton and Axl performed Freddie Mercury's most popular song, "Bohemian Rhapsody," to thousands of supporters and fans.

Elton John, here with singer Bonnie Raitt, was honored for his charity work and AIDS activism at the Grammy MusiCares Dinner in February 2000.

Back on the Rise

With the release of the album *Duets*, 1992 was becoming another career highlight for Elton. The album was composed of collaborations with other artists. Tammy Wynette, RuPaul, Leonard Cohen, Bonnie Raitt, and many other famous singers joined Elton on the album. It is no wonder then that Warner/Chappell Music offered Elton and Bernie a contract for $39 million that year, the largest cash advance in music publishing history.

Tragedy and the Future

After an astounding year in 1992, Elton was back on top, doing incredibly well in his personal and professional life. His proactive work for AIDS, with the Elton John AIDS Foundation and benefit concerts, brought him a satisfaction that meant more than commercial and financial success. In an interview on the BBC aired on March

30, 1997, Elton shared how growing older meant growing more peaceful: "I quite like being by myself sometimes. Just to zone out at home. I never used to be good at that. I used to have to have people around me. The older you get the more tolerant you become to being alone."

The Lion King

In 1993, Elton began to work with Disney Studios and Tim Rice on the score for an upcoming Disney movie called *The Lion King*. The film was a touching story about a young lion's struggle to grow and learn about the world. The story's main focus was on the relationship between father and son. Elton and Tim worked for months on the music, and finally came up with songs they loved. "Circle of Life" was their favorite.

In 1994, when the movie hit theaters, audiences everywhere loved it, in particular the movie's sound track. The album made it to number one on the U.S. charts, a rare accomplishment for a movie sound track.

Rock and Roll Hall of Fame Honors

In 1994, Elton received one the greatest rewards a rock and roller can receive: He was inducted into the Rock and Roll Hall of Fame. As the Hall of Fame cited, there are few performers who have been in rock as long as Elton. In 1992, Elton beat out Elvis Presley's old record for the most years in a row of top-40 hits on *Billboard*'s singles chart. Elton had been on the charts every year since the entry of "Your Song" in the late '70s. Even before 1994, Elton was a legend. Being inducted into the Hall of Fame formally acknowledged him as a musician who added his own style to rock and roll and therefore helped keep its captivating sound thriving.

Tragedy Strikes

The past few years for Elton had been amazing ones. He was invigorated with his successes and he was flying high with the public's appreciation. Then, on July 15, 1997, one of the fashion

Did You Know?

March 25, 1997, was Elton John's fiftieth birthday, and he was ready to party. The quirky Elton John arrived at his huge party dressed as Marie Antoinette, the queen whose famous line, "Let them eat cake," has been engraved into world history. Can you guess what Elton sang as he walked through the door of his party dressed as extravagantly as the queen? He sang, "Let them eat cake!"

world's biggest leaders was murdered outside of his home in Florida. On that day, Gianni Versace was shot dead by Andrew Cunanan. Elton John and Gianni Versace had been friends for years, and Elton experienced tremendous pain from the loss of his dear friend. His close friend, Diana, Princess of Wales, comforted the weeping Elton at Versace's funeral.

The cover for the specially rewritten version of "Candle in the Wind"

Only a few months later, on August 31, 1997, the world lost another beloved figure: Princess Diana. She perished in an automobile accident in Paris, France. While just a few months earlier, Elton had cried in her arms at Versace's funeral, he now had to prepare himself to play the piano at hers.

Elton was overcome with enormous grief when he heard of Diana's death. Yet Elton wanted to pay tribute to this woman who had fought so hard as a humanitarian, especially in her fight for AIDS sufferers. In an interview with Barbara Walters before Diana's funeral, Elton spoke of his plan to see that she would never be forgotten: "In England they have been showing montages of Diana with 'Candle in the Wind,' which was a song that Bernie Taupin and I wrote about Marilyn Monroe. So rather than sing that, which I think is totally inappropriate because it's a song about Marilyn Monroe, I asked Bernie to write a brand new lyric. The first line is 'Goodbye, England's rose.'"

Princess Diana's death was a shock, and Elton decided that after he played "England's Rose" at her funeral he would never play it publicly again. On the day of her funeral, much of the world watched. Diana had been popular because she loved and took care of the sick and less fortunate. As Elton sat down to play his good-bye message to Diana, he said he thought, "When I started singing and playing, I suddenly realized this was it. I was fairly composed all the way through and I sang it well. But at the beginning of the last verse my voice cracked and I was really chock-full of emotion and I had to close my eyes and grit my teeth and get through it."

Elton donated all proceeds from "England's Rose" to a memorial fund in Princess Diana's

Elton John arrives at Westminster Abbey for Princess Diana's funeral with David Furnish, his longtime partner.

name that would go to charity. The single made it to number one on both American and British charts. It is his highest-selling single to date.

Finding Peace and Moving On

Recovering from the death of a loved one is a long process, and Elton was recovering from the deaths of two loved ones. However, unlike in the past when he let himself sink into depression, Elton directed his attention not to his pain but to how he could use this experience to help teach others.

Knighthood

On February 24, 1998, Elton John received a knighthood for his contribution to music and his AIDS fund-raising. His name from that moment forward has been Sir Elton John. What exactly does a knighthood entail? It is basically a sign of honor and loyalty to one's country. Elton, through his music and influence as a star, helped better the United Kingdom—the knighthood honors him for this.

In 2000, Elton John realized a lifelong dream when *Aida*, his musical cowritten with Tim Rice, opened on Broadway.

Aida

It had always been Elton's dream to write a musical. In 2000, the musical *Aida* opened on Broadway and created waves of excitement throughout the world. The musical is based on Verdi's famous opera, *Aida,* but it includes rock and roll as well. The music was recorded by a variety of artists, from Leann Rimes to Boyz II Men. The members of Boyz II Men had this to say about being asked to work with Elton on the sound track: "Our instant response was 'Really?!' The whole Elton John experience was really cool with us. Just the fact that somebody as respected as him believed in us—not only to sing the song, but also to produce it—was a privilege."

The Present and into the Future

In 2001, Elton released his thirty-fifth album, called *Songs from the West Coast.* He is still working with Bernie Taupin, who wrote the lyrics for this most recent album, as well as the lyrics for

John's last thirty-three albums. Amazingly, Elton and Bernie found in one another a special bond, an equation for success and good music. Few people are lucky enough to stumble upon such a startling combination and even fewer are able to greet continuous success because of it. Neither musician, when they started out in small towns with big dreams, would have guessed their present accomplishments. That's why wherever Elton heads in the future will undoubtedly bring more legendary music from a legendary man.

SELECTED DISCOGRAPHY

1969 *Empty Sky*
1970 *Elton John*
1970 *Tumbleweed Connection*
1971 *11-17-70*
1971 *Friends*
1971 *Madman Across the Water*
1972 *Honky Chateau*
1973 *Goodbye Yellow Brick Road*
1974 *Caribou*
1978 *A Single Man*
1980 *21 at 33*
1982 *Jump Up!*
1984 *Breaking Hearts*
1985 *Ice on Fire*
1986 *Leather Jackets*
1988 *Reg Strikes Back*
1989 *Sleeping with the Past*
1992 *The One*
1995 *Made in England*
1997 *The Big Picture*
2000 *One Night Only*
2001 *Songs from the West Coast*

GLOSSARY

acclimate To adapt to an environment or lifestyle; to feel comfortable in a situation.

AIDS/HIV AIDS is a disease caused by HIV, human immunodeficiency virus, which breaks down the body's immune system until it can no longer fight off even minor illnesses, such as the common cold.

booking manager A person who is in charge of finding a band places to play.

estrangement Indifference where there had formerly been love, affection, or friendliness; a separation.

gaudy Marked by dazzling brilliance, showiness, or extravagance.

hemophiliac A person whose blood does not clot, causing the person to be at high risk of death from small injuries because they cause extensive bleeding.

hiatus A break or vacation.

idol A person or object that is looked up to for representing or symbolizing an idea that is appreciated, like bravery or intelligence.

musical prodigy A child who can play an instrument with little or no instruction.

octave A musical tone, often used to describe the pitch of someone's voice.

pessimistic Having a cynical or gloomy attitude, marked by the belief that the worst will happen.

prejudice A negative and hostile attitude directed against an individual, a group, or a race for their supposed characteristics.

proactive Acting in anticipation of future problems and working for change.

rock and roll Popular music usually played on electronically amplified instruments, known for its accented beats, repetition of simple phrases, and often country, folk, and blues elements.

sheet music Single sheets of paper printed on one or both sides that display a song's notes; used by musicians to lead them through the notes of a song.

trade magazine A magazine that covers and reviews specific topics in detail, such as music or literature.

TO FIND OUT MORE

Elton John AIDS Foundation
P.O. Box 17139
Beverly Hills, CA 90209-3139
(310) 535-1775
Web site: http://www.ejaf.org

Hercules—International Elton John Fan Club
c/o Barb Crowley Madruga
P.O. Box 692392
Orlando, FL 32869-2392
e-mail: HerculesUSA@eltonfan.net
Web site: http://www.eltonfan.net

Rock and Roll Hall of Fame and Museum
One Key Plaza
Cleveland, OH 44114
(888) 764-ROCK (7625)
Web site: http://www.rockhall.com

Web Sites

Due to the changing nature of Internet links, the Rosen Publishing Group, Inc., has developed an online list of Web sites related to the subject of this book. This site is updated regularly. Please use this link to access the list:

http://www.rosenlinks.com/rrhf/ejon/

FOR FURTHER READING

Bernardin, Claude, and Tom Stanton. *Rocket Man.* Westport, CT: Greenwood Press, 1995.

Bright, Spense. *The Essential Elton John.* London: Chameleon Publishing, 2001.

Cass, Caroline. *Elton John Flower Fantasy.* London: George Weidenfeld & Nicolson Ltd., 1997.

Clarke, Gary. *Elton My Elton.* London: Smith Gryphon Limited, 1995.

Heatley, Michael. *The Life and Music of a Legendary Performer.* London: CLB International, 1998.

Lassell, Michael, and Tim Rice. *Elton John and Tim Rice's* Aida*: Bringing the Broadway Show to Life.* New York: Hyperion, 2000.

Rosenthal, Elizabeth. *His Song: The Musical Journey of Elton John.* London: Billboard Books, 2001.

Works Cited

Cromer, Ben. "Producer Dudgeon's Flair Felt Beyond His Elton Classics." *Billboard,* April 26, 1997.

"The Rock Family Affair." *Life*, September 24, 1971.

Bauder, David. Times Herald-Record Online. "Elton John's New 'Candle in the Wind' to Be Released as Charity Single." Retrieved February 2002.

Sischy, Ingrid. "AIDA." *Interview*, April 1999.

Street-Porter, Janet. "As the Crow Flies—Country Comfort." BBC2 TV, April 3, 1997.

Towne, Terry. "Elton John Talks." *Jazz & Pop*, January 1971.

20/20, ABC News. "Elton John." September 5, 1997.

Welch, Chris. *Melody Maker*, December 21, 1974.

INDEX

CREDITS

About the Author

Katherine White is a production editor and a freelance writer. She lives in Brooklyn, New York.

Photo Credits

Cover, pp. 4, 5, 13, 18–19, 22, 25, 32, 40–41, 44, 46, 48, 58, 60, 62, 66, 72, 76, 78, 82, 86, 88, 90, 96, 98 © Corbis; pp. 7, 10, 94 © AP/Wide World Photos.

Editor

Eliza Berkowitz

Design

Thomas Forget

Layout

Nelson Sá